Arranging Nature

Arranging Nature

Paul Naylor

Chax Press
Tucson 2006

Parts one and three of this book were published as a chapbook by Potato Clock Press; part two appeared in *Hambone,* and part five appeared in *The Cultural Society.* Many thanks to the editors of those venues for their support.

Thanks to Max Bertola (www.so-utah.com) for the use of his photograph of "The Holy Ghost and Companions" on the cover.

ISBN 0-925904-54-6

Chax Press
101 West Sixth Street
Tucson, Arizona 85701

This and other projects by Chax Press are supported by the Tucson Pima Arts Council and by the Arizona Commission on the Arts with funding from the State of Arizona and the National Endowment for the Arts.

Arizona Commission on the Arts

TUCSON PIMA ARTS COUNCIL

NATIONAL ENDOWMENT FOR THE ARTS

For Debi Kilb

And so the atoms swerve a little—they must . . .

Lucretius

Is it not maimed and imperfect nature that I am conversant with?

Henry David Thoreau

One

1

Mother of delight,
sweet wheeling sign,
rouse sea and
all we breathe
and begotten rise to light;
from winds flee
storm's artful
ocean
and calm become.
When wide for spring and splendor
fostering blows free,
pricked power of air
you enter
fertile beast
(so seized
wherever you lead);
across hungering
homes and fields,
heart struck lure
desire their kind.
You alone
since
shores of light,
I try
to pen
my friend
accomplished
grace!

2

Or when our eyes groveling
under religion's dust
(thrust of horrible face
glowering to die),
a mortal dared
defy
fables nor
rumble all the more
whetted mind
to open nature.
Vigor strode far,
the world
raided unmeasured all
with knowledge of what can rise
or cannot grant its own
finite scope or
lies of trampled
gods.

3

Why too bloom in spring, ripen in summer,
or pour forth its urging of autumn,
unless each thing
in time reveals
which earth will bear
so tender is light
from nothing once sprung
out of all haphazard,
nor be blocked
from
whatever would need no time
if
presto!
leaps the earth full-grown.
None we know
grow from a certain
preserve
and nourished by matter
could never
its lusty
rains
alive.

4

Further force would crush
all matter
more or less
would kill
whose intertwining
severs
unlike
itself
comes
to destroy.
Nothing shatters
all,
rain passes,
pours down,
corn swells forth
and trees heavy with fruit.
From these we and beasts
come bustling
bird's song;
fields having fed,
glistening dew
drips
on unsteady
heads, tender
to nothing nature restores
nor allows.

5

So empty
would cease
which
at all times
could advance
and yield.
But heights of sky
before our eyes move
by void
not lack
could never
everywhere rest.
No matter
has gaps:
Water will
and within
every body
grows
lowest roots
rise in
sounds flutter and fly right
to the bone.
But
by means things
weigh,
though
no more
should same
bodies press
and persist in
equal light
inside
certain
emptiness
scented reason sought.

6

Let me weave poetry
of things
in themselves
move and scatter.
The senses we share,
first founded on
grounds of hidden
inquiry,
we call void
nowhere
or wandering ways
demonstrated.

And
free or sheltered
helped compose
whatever would be.
If you touch slightly or softly,
add to it
a bodily thing.
But if any
could bar
space,
whatever
itself
or being
lacks,
matter
can be admitted
beside
our senses
grasp.

7

Now if nature
by time's ravages
had reduced
nothing
conceived and
shattered more easily
restored.
Infinite ages
undoing
too little time to
limit splitting
we see
seasons
flower and

solid
explains soft things too
come to be
by power and persist;
since
beginning
by no means
nature would lack
a first
thriving
simplicity
to show its strength.

8

To proceed
we perceive
each point remains
minimal
and is
something else
after
crowded order
since they
cling no force can pry them free.
Then solid,
tight-packed parts
not brought
in everlasting
stripped or diminished
saved these seeds,
the smallest
you imagine
infinitely
into no end!

9

So who
of fire alone,
fallen from truth,
enters a
cryptic style—
who seeks
what
lurks under twisted words
tickles their ears
with pretty sound.
For how various
fire
rarefies and condenses
bright
qualities they compose.
Force fiercer than heat;
scatter or split,
no further effects can follow
from two
alone.
This void
could be
Muses seem so
shy,
so fearing they lose the true
nor free of
their world would make
one from
ablaze slings light and smoke:
It cannot be composed.

10

First among these,
the wide-whorled sprays
of green waves
and divides
from grumbling
wrath
and violent flames
flashing
wonders,
they say,
well fortified with
excellence,
most wondrous to be loved
for godlike song
in verse
not born of human stock.

11

Yet
inferior
oracles give
of discovery,
reason
utters
their ruin
comes crashing
void
and penetrable
air
of bodies
err
no end
in things.
(Observe around us
utterly far
we infer
a liminal minimum.)

12

But often
of towering
force until
flash in open flame
is laced with
seeds of heat
set blazing.
But if hidden deep
could never
level and reduce to ash
what saying
depends on
arranging
to
create?
These words
are made of change in
flame.
Believe
your eyes exist,
endowed with
death,
struck
wet with tears!
Now know what remains:
A dark
prophet's heart,
stinging sweet Muse
charged
the trackless haunts
untrodden.

13

Neither sea nor field
nor mortal
moment
wrenched free from
drift
have
scattered to combine.
For assigning
order to
questions of
shuffled and jumbled
time driven
chance
at last an arrangement
would create
so many
should
brim and spill
the warm
new brood to
bloom.

14

Lest the world
loosen through
and disasters follow
thunderous fall
and flees
emptiness among
ruins
fraying
space and blind
first
annihilation's
rush

will guide
nor
read
nature's knowledge.

Two

1

Condense and collapse, cloud in cloud, an embryonic sun forms nebula, forms gas accretes and gathers in turbulent swirling birth.

So composed of starroot, Earth hurtles through firmament.

Home sweet home—a cold rock compiled of iron, silicon, magnesium, aluminum, and oxygen.

What a thought we once had, just before dawn, the sun a rumor soon to be fact.

Was it a garden we recalled or a night so dark death would mean reprieve? Was it of a snake hissing or of one become two, thickening the plot?

2

Memory elides the opening scene, origin of all.

Neither animal nor vegetable, the first trackless mass no man has trod.

Unremittent days ravaged beyond record left in rock. Imagine aggregates of minerals—inorganic crystalline core composed of olivine, augite, pyrite; quartz, feldspar, clay; calcite, dolomite, gold.

Left more than a quarry in silent remains.

Fracture's asymmetrical surface.

Fire's reflected light.

3

Years Ago	Event
4.6 Billion	Earth Formed
3.6 Billion	Oldest Fossils
700 Million	First Multicellular Animals
510 Million	First Fish
430 Million	First Land Plants
360 Million	First Amphibians
230 Million	First Dinosaurs
222 Million	First Mammals
145 Million	First Birds
115 Million	First Flowering Plants
66 Million	Dinosaurs Become Extinct
53 Million	First Horses
4 Million	First Humans
1.6 Million	Ice Age Begins
10,000	Ice Age Ends
9,873	Writing Invented
Today	Wrote This

4

Fireformed of molten rock beneath the Earth's surface. Magma arrayed in mineral crystals cools and becomes igneous above and below all we know.

Disgorged by volcanoes, rhyolite, andesite, and basalt cool above. Granite, diorite, and gabbro cool below, waiting to make mountains rise and slice the sky.

I grew up surrounded by granite. Mountains made of it. Temples and banks built of it. Schools and stores named after it.

God's Word lies locked in a granite vault up Little Cottonwood Canyon, southeast of Salt Lake City. At twelve, I thought that might be true.

5

Arcuate scarp surrounded by scree. Rock worn by wind and what little rain there is.

Eroding starroot. Rainshadowed slope.

So much composed of sediment left by the sea in the Mesozoic. Sandstone, silt, clay, and shale.

Like a life layered on a page, each clause an epoch undone.

200 million year-old Tyrannosaurus teeth and Pterodactyl wings concealed in rock read by fossil light.

No one there to write this down. An afterthought unearthed.

Or to witness the birth of the Uinta Mountains in the Paleocene or watch the Wasatch Mountains rise 5000 feet in the Miocene.

Perhaps a few crouched by firelight as the ice age draws to a close.

6

Known to us as their adversaries knew them, as Ancestral Enemies or Anasazi, in Navajo. Known to their descendants, the Hopi, as Hisatsinom or The Old Ones.

What they made of nature—a basket woven from windblown reed, an arrowhead chipped from obsidian.

And what nature made of them—antelope hunter, root seeker, water monger wandering seep to seep.

Been and gone by the time Columbus came. Lithic scatter in tamarisk grove. Mute ruins carved in alcoves facing south. Low doorway leads where?

Abrade.

Adumbrate.

Art of inner eye.

7

Saw in southern Utah petroglyphs two thousand years old etched by tribes whose ancestors arrived twelve thousand years before Brigham Young said this is the place.

After erosion exposed the deep we see as surface unearthed. Below becomes above. Before becomes present and hindsight sees history best.

Except our own blinded by firelight.

Look in, he said.

Nothing there, I replied.

Concordant sill, discordant dike—each beneath our feet.

At sixteen, stood dumbstruck before bighorn sheep incised in rock at Nine Mile Canyon.

8

Navajo, Ute, Piute, and Shoshoni followed Fremont and Anasazi followed nameless nomads into the rock they wrote.

Descend here, where history draws a blank. Crawled in caves toward an uncertain source they wrote.

Behind what we see. Art of inner eye incised in limestone. Adumbrated outcome omitted from what they wrote.

Cave of ancient eye cut from cliff face concealed from sight. Crawled on all fours memory informs me. It was I wrote.

9

Wind-troubled waters made Pe-mish and Pa-ha make more until too many became. A great fog covered the valley and all were lost, wandering off to live in other lands.

So old, no one knows who told it.

Rock speaks only of its own. The lines left by Lake Bonneville, for instance. Easy reading from the window I was raised behind.

Looked out on what I didn't know from where I did.

Mount Olympus etched in my mind elides the opening scene.

What once was shore is not.

Look out.

10

There's a story I can't recall of nameless wandering the region. At eighteen, what else could be expected?

Imagine a bridge between Asia and Alaska exposed in the Pleistocene—then roamed this way. That's our story.

Theirs is they came up from below. Cave of ancient eye incised. Hunt for mammoths, bison, and tapirs abraded. Annihilated tale of inner world untold.

Crawled back in the cave. On all fours when I was young. Others at ease.

Paleo-people at home on hurtling Earth.

Firelight turned inside out.

Quarry concurs.

11

With the glaciers gone and the world dried up, five thousand years before Christ and seven thousand before Brigham Young set foot in the state, nomads gathered wild plants and hunted small game, wove baskets and carved wood, scored rock with abstract suns, snakes, and birds.

Signs of rite? Territorial warnings? Appeasing above or below?

What once was sure is not.

Ask the inner eye.

Beware, traveler. Horned gods rule here.

Look in.

12

Travel south from Price on Utah 10 toward the San Rafael Swell. Turn east on Buckhorn Wash Road, about a mile north of Castle Dale. (BLM sign reads "Pictograph Panel 22.") Drive seventeen miles on unpaved road, then turn south. After crossing a cattle guard eight miles in, park on the north side of the road and hike three miles down the canyon.

Painted red, yellow, and beige on sandstone walls. Jackal-headed snake strikes one-armed man. Sinister figures with sticks block the way. Faceless, winged anthropomorphs of ancient eye.

And then went down in dream, slithered between rocks as snakethought released.

Or up in firmament unearthed, birdword lament unleashed.

13

Oddly angled shadow. Sun undone. Crossed mesa top, downdrift to valley. Rich in red rock, pink rock, yellow and white rock.

Felt myself a speck, not spectacle. Alone in trivial defeat. All of twenty-one and thought myself undone. What doesn't care brings comfort. Irrelevance brought to close focus.

The Virgin River cut through 2000 feet of pink and white sandstone, leaving Zion Canyon in its wake as more than a place for me to take center stage.

Which dream had come to an end—and which was beginning? I know the answer now. But then went down to despair.

Eroding slope. Windrippled rock.

Thickened plot not my own to etch on stone.

Beveled crossbed of silt and clay. Hanging garden high on canyon wall.

14

Home sweet home—a comfortable house in the suburbs. Paneled bedroom in the basement. Happy family upstairs. I've always been afraid to write that sentence. Who wants to hear it?

Looked out from where I was.

Mount Olympus towers over the valley. Canyon breeze eases summer's heat. Pyracantha and pine in front, Russian olive and apple in back.

Look out from where I am.

Bare trees in New Jersey winter. I'll fly home this spring and drive from Salt Lake to Zion, cut east to Monument Valley, work my way north through Canyonlands and Arches, then back to the Wasatch Range that frames my life.

Someone here to write this down.

An I incised.

Three

1

How sweet the wind-whipped struggle
and sweet the lines of peril
dwelling in truth straying
for rank and toil

O heart how squandered
not our nature alone but our bodies need
and sooth will spread demand in hand
with gold become and lie at ease
in luxury's rule of reason

unless spurring shores of far-flung care
and fear pierce bright splendor of power
in darkness lurking light more terrible
will come not by sun
but scattered by law

2

Listen what brings force to birth
makes restless whirl through space

Together we see silent
and awake to watch all ages persist
when reason falls away
diminished nor renewed grows greater

Now begetting new has erred
through unknown weight
creates and bound together
each instant so solid with nothing behind

3

All tossed and tumbled
memory's reach might span
unmeasured forever in all directions
and wonder never rests
in depths untried chasm
of veer and jar tangled and entwined
to splendor's end

Of shadow or semblance
hovering shade of flecks mingle
among themselves never assailed
secession tossed and traced rays of turmoil
hidden invisible lash scattering
(things closest to force) and thrust

4

With few words   dappled birds
   flutter and fill   untracked song
      risen sun shining   to strike
   not one   but woven among each
and nothing beyond   ferries faster than time

   Nor can they follow   the law
governs all   matter says   nature needs
   to turn urges   tease us to dream
far from reason   knew nothing
   nor dare assert   this world made
      to untangle

5

No power   fooled by flames
seize the trees
and weigh them down   nor thinking leaps
to lick from below

Shot body flashes   deeper we plunge
in fire   nature gives way to light
(bends toward earth)   through cloud-torn
skirmish they fall

But who believes   can beget
collisions rise to life   far from truth
and reason drops   through thin air
routed by   emptiness
can't yield

6

Therefore   matter must quiet
emptiness from above   and engender nature
to swerve the slightest   seems to refute
a thing aslant can see   and ascertain

Then if all linked   from old arising fate
for eternity   will wrest from pleasure
leads no place   the mind has swept
the will impels an instant   open and eager

while spurned every limb   striving desire sees first
the heart of another bridle   against headlong flight
the multitude reigned in and granted   an inborn power
prevents any inner press   and bears
the tiniest swerve of time

7

The wealth of matter
spread so thin   dies possessed
and ever thrives   as nature
escapes   to flee the source   a new force
might rise   and alter all

which should astonish
yet stands in peace   proper to each
never sees   wonder intervene
with bejeweled dew

shines   white glow on green
glittering thunder   shouts and shaking
still   one steady gleam

8

Understand how far they diverge
and assume in wonder there's wealth
beyond limit taught to reason
won't mold soundless sleek
and dappled brood untracked breed

Blood alone will roam cloven with dew
and brim of burden knows nature intervenes
soft waves slake the same
bound for form hurtles shape

Quick light tight fire
risen from tinder thin light of water
or wine olive or atoms
sifted to seep one by one

9

Honey tongue   twist of taste
smooth and compose
sense with pleasure   seems stitched
and split   our slashing

Finally to touch   each shape
nerves nimble as life
nor think a corpse   on altar of spice
nor say which eyes   wring and repel
what caresses sense
or possesses   bent to bruise
each issues forth   from jumble and jar
far various

And what interlocked
tangled   adamant in contempt
of brazen strike and fly   like smoke
not formed   from free
things arise

10

But that bitter   sweat for wonder
since it's smooth   and crude
the sea's acrimony   trickles through
leaves   and seeds

To what limits   need be forgiven
new shapes   shuffling logic and form
endless impossible gleaming   delight lies
in myrrh   and honey scorned song
sun scorched measures
in stiffening wind

11

What links   first beginnings
made infinite shapes   of finite forms
in verse   uphold endless
invasion so vast   in fertile birth
found matter   begotten and bound
to be engendered through all   by force
in swirling sea of foreign alliance
scatters hull and prow   sail and oar
overcome to shun   traitors
lure with limit   hurl in truce

So lethal prevails   in perpetual increase
creatures locked for all   force
put to flight   song mingled with light

12

These lines should seal   nothing
          not jumbled   and numerous in kind
replenished   fire arises   (earth's fury)
          glossy beasts   roam rivers and trees

          Earth alone   formed the flesh
of poets old and sang   lashing this world
                    hangs and obeys   bound with a crown
          so symboled over awe   an idol rides

          ancient rite   first law drawn taut
                    in frenzy signs of fury   in thankless
          quake with fear   in rhythm gleaming
                    Greeks call Jove's wail
          on brazen wound   ingeniously presented
                              reason rejects

13

For necessity above eternity
in highest peace withdrawn
from sorrow free of need
not won by rage

Fact never felt
wealth of first beginning
sun insists on sea and wine gives way
to truth and taint

And grazing on plain of horned heaven
thirst to preserve nature as blood in vein
heat in heart fire in mind
must smuggle light to life
ashes to logic hidden in seeds shaped as verse
many words must confess a few
common to all nor two alike

14

Link every way   and race would spring
as branches sprout with life   feeds flame
as fixed law to each   brings unseen bonds
held fast by form   as tangle divides
land and sea   holds heaven back

Listen   and heed love
search for dazzle born   of any color
since all minds go astray   and blind
before sunlight   joins in darkness
immutable world   reduced to change
beyond limit   earliest taint
returns to one   stunning hue

Four

1

September 2. No pose. Just write as if it's possible to be without guise. As if that's what I'm after.

A few pages ago, it was winter and I was living in New Jersey. Now it's summer and we've moved back to San Diego.

Where will the weeds be when I'm gone? The flowers can take care of themselves—but what about the weeds?

Guile is close to guise, but both are matters of posture and cunning, though the latter hides the former's candor.

In our complex, sprinklers set themselves off at 9:46 PM no matter what. People by the pool drink and sing; I sit and surf, pleased to be among them.

Take I-5 to Encinitas Boulevard, the website says. Go half a mile east and turn left on Quail Gardens Drive—entrance on the left.

The moon obscures the deck lights below, though the swimmers seem not to notice.

Sprinklers sound like my childhood.

2

September 3. The mission of Quail Botanical Gardens Foundation, Inc. a 501 (c) (3) nonprofit organization, is to actively participate in the conservation of rare, threatened and endangered plant species, to serve the botanical and horticulture needs of San Diego County, and to exist as an urban retreat.

Can a fence keep people out or nature in?

One runs along the edge of exhibits arranged according to climate: Desert, Tropical, Subtropical, Mediterranean.

San Diego is classified as Mediterranean in general and Coastal Sage Scrub in particular.

One of the most threatened habitats in the United States.

Jacaranda and ice cream bean are my favorite names from today's tour. Globe artichoke sounds good too and is in bloom today on the QBG website. My favorite phrase is tucked back among weaver's bamboo.

Who knew a fig is a fruit?

The complex we live in has a faux-Italian electronic gate, the remote for which I continually forget. That theme runs throughout the structure.

I like walking in and out of it.

3

September 5. So here we are, happy to be back in this seaside desert where winter happens on a Wednesday.

Hope we can qualify for the jumbo loan.

The Gardens are right where we left them, though the Overlook Pavilion is new and beautifully done.

You can see the ocean from up here. It's much bigger than I imagine. But does the shore signify its beginning or its end? Either way, fear keeps me out and sharks in.

Science shows pools present fewer problems—particularly when management keeps them clean. Sharks and sewage spills are rarely reported.

I want to know the names for all kinds of flora before I die, beginning with subtropical fruits and ending with Adorno.

None of these poems should end on a bleak note, so let's agree that hydrangeas remind us all of Hostess Snowballs and call it a day.

4

September 6. The palm trees are all in place. They trucked them in four months ago and stuck them where they belong. I'll get to watch that happen when they finish building the northern wing of our complex.

One of the most threatened habitats in the United States.

The bulldozer is the honorary bird of Southern California.

From the Overlook you can see them grading vast tracts of land for another cluster of Apartment Resort Homes like the one we live in. I'm not sure what the solution is, but anyone who moves here is part of the problem.

That means us.

The Quail Botanical Gardens were once home to Charles and Ruth Larabee, collectors of exotic plants and trees, which they arranged on a twenty-six acre private garden. After Ruth dumped Chuck (or was it the other way around?), she turned it over to San Diego County in 1957 to be preserved and developed as a plant and wildlife sanctuary.

Donations are tax deductible.

That means us.

5

September 7. Who knew nature was on a need to know basis?

Guilt is close to guise. It's the next off ramp, in fact.

To refresh your memory, turn east on Encinitas Boulevard and follow the signs on the right pointing left.

You cain't miss it is a phrase often heard down South.

They have nature there too, but it's arranged by different geologic and economic effects. Money may make the world go round, but tectonic plates make it shake. Both are particularly true in our new neighborhood.

We went to the Memphis Botanic Gardens two or three times a year, especially in the spring, when the dogwoods and azaleas explode with beauty.

These are cedar trees; those are tamarisk.

It's easy to get confused.

6

September 8. Can oleander grow away from the freeway? Can a dragon tree live without reason? Do sewage spills have feelings too?

These are questions binge-eating at Roberto's can't cover up. Nor can the pathetic fallacy whisk them away.

The docent-in-training told us worm gold was just worm poop and no one should pay too much for it. She seemed to think herself rakish for saying so.

I suspect a hidden teleology at work in naming those orange and white flowers angel's trumpets.

White-leaved rock rose grows up then out of its own accord.

I left believing the African tulip tree, its reddish-orange flowers in full bloom, the most beautiful of all.

They should clone a few for the complex.

7

September 10. Some sentences are parasites; others are epiphytes. It's easy to get confused. Examples of the latter are the orchids growing on the jacaranda next to the gift shop.

Philodendron is easier to say than spell. It's the opposite with chrysanthemum.

I'm afraid to ask what the mission is behind the mission-style architecture dominating my view.

Are these poems parasites or epiphytes? Do they grow off or with experience? Do they supply their own nutrients or take from others?

I doubt this is what Kierkegaard had in mind when he spoke of the teleological suspension of the ethical, but it is what I had in mind when I spoke of the ethical suspension of the teleological.

Someone smart said art should raise rather than answer questions.

I can live with or off that.

8

September 11. There will never be enough flowers.

9

September 12. Yesterday, while thousands waited for trading to begin, drinking coffee, logging on, talking to friends about their kids or the Yankees-Red Sox rainout the night before.

What tone wouldn't conceal a pose? What prayer could I offer—and to whom or what?

A wreath of words can't turn a market into a garden.

All at a loss.

I imagine a man my age, reaching across a desk to straighten a picture of his wife. I imagine all the replays she'll try not to watch.

10

September 19. The unconscionable acts perpetrated on this past September 11 have left the world stunned. Quail Botanical Gardens extends its sincerest sympathies to the very many people who have suffered injuries and lost loved ones in this horrible act.

We would like to provide an open invitation for as many people as possible to visit the Gardens, as we all need an opportunity to cope with and start to heal after this tragic event. Therefore, while donations will be accepted, the public is invited to visit free of charge for one month starting Sunday, September 16 through Sunday, October 14.

Dead man's tree: toxic sap, regarded as evil by indigenous Africans.

The sweet smell of angel's trumpet conceals poisonous seed. Oleander bears the same fate.

About two million years ago, oxygen assaulted the atmosphere, destroying almost all forms of life. But what once was poison made possible the evolution of nuclei in cells, which made possible anything that sucks down air, including me.

The notion of no bleak notes is long gone. Fearful days before us.

Yellow milkbrush. Laurel leaf. Tea-oil tree. Bird of paradise passed its bloom. Kirta, King of Bitters presides.

Lured by beauty. Long wait for sense.

11

September 20. What's behind this Bush? Who's arranging nature in such terrifying ways?

Tear it up, root and branch. Eliminate cells. Inoculate us against evil. Those are the answers I'm told.

The questions, though, concern the worship of comfort.

Ease is all. Eucalyptus trees wave in agreement.

All habitats are threatened today.

Behind the pattern is a trace. Behind the trace is a sign separating the Old World Desert Garden from the New.

Succulents on one side; aloe on the other.

12

September 21. This poem's in memory of my mom. She died five years ago today.

Red and white carnations were her favorites. My dad put a dozen of each on her grave today, something he does every year on her birthday and their anniversary too.

They were best friends.

Absence is anything but empty. It's filled with all we miss.

I never thought I'd miss two office buildings.

Where will the people who loved all the people we'll never find put flowers?

13

September 27. The questions now concern what belongs where and what to do about what doesn't.

Most of what I see doesn't. The complex I live in is part of a larger complex, which is part of an even larger complex, which extends to the ends of the earth, I'm afraid.

And most of what I see in the Garden doesn't belong. The Larabees and those who followed hauled it all in from somewhere else—much to their credit and my pleasure.

But do our ships and planes and pumps belong where they are? Are they threatened or threatening? And what do they conserve?

The Old World Desert Garden needs less water than many believe.

Aloe grows on its own.

14

September 29. Coyote bush belongs.

Honeysuckle and saltbrush belong.

Engleman oak, mountain mahogany, big-berry manzanita—mescalito and mesquite, indigo and celosa belong.

Desert lavender, blue-candle cacti, black cottonwood—elderberry and ironwood, sedge and ephedra belong.

Prickly pear and bottlebrush belong.

And live-forever belongs.

Black mission fig falls from its tree, free of the guile or guilt of those who brought its kind to San Diego in 1769.

Up at the Pavilion, it's hard to overlook either the ocean to the west or the land cleared for building to the east.

What lies between?

Five

1

Darkrise
deep song,
sunder uncut
phrase and page,
bedecked golden life
and godlike beings flutter;
windlash broken beneath
each eyesnarled heart,
each ensnared shape
trembles beside
fear lurking
larkstar.

2

Birdword lament,
broken scriptsite song,
feel veer reverse
in soft sleep tumble
limbseed release
lingers after idle care.

Leaves flee from trees,
breathless bears
bones to sudden shore,
unseen caress of
soul crossed sense stolen
and staggers on.

Lashdanced ear,
spurred eyestalk sight,
parted peace
of evanescent weight,
winebound bier
awaits its scent of flesh.

Nothing simpler than
power undone,
empty threat abandoned,
burning bone
on marrow skin shield,
thriving tongue.

3

Thymeless tempting eye
stirs ear and blood
becomes force.
Jumbled
warmth
of breathbeat,
heart sweeps wide
and mingles myrrh with

each enraptured word
taken by eternity.
Flickering leaf
quivers
in calm
air like quiet
anonymous lies
told toward archaic bliss.

4

Denied the soul diffused,
the whole dazzled
distress clings to slender
thread, thistledown
trapped in a spider's web.

When fettered by final design,
cold chill of mirthless
world remains an untold tale,
a windtossed dirge
of torn and scattered leaves.

But song struck from flint
of fleeting time
inflames each word secure
in mind's ripe eye,
attuned to heartsharp ear.

A weed's reward, he said;
a good omen greets
a flower's return in Spring,
a thing seen as light
eclipsed by shadow's edge.

5

Thin
reed
sings

wind
whisks
away

body
blind
soul.

6

Sheltered
song larkspur
listens

lapsed
bitterroot reason
hesitates

to say
windshaken
whole

in
a gust of old
skin.

7

Broken soul
of force
fed on desire—

which hawk swoops
to doveless
trembling death?

Sullen stalkseed
reprive
of weltered sky—

which cloud carries
the bolt
that burns the tree?

Death stalks love's
heedless
reprive of hope—

stammering soul
swoops
to stunned reply.

8

So whose violent
brood decries
thought as flight?

And whose foolish
heart denies
a flower its end?

I have none but
scuffling lines
in lieu of truth,

in place of power
left at last
to mortal spoils—

a surge of words
alert to lies
everlasting as

eternity decrees
an untamed
life breaks free.

9

Stricken
song begins in
strife

gnaws
hollow reason
away

leaves
all that's left
broken

bones
picked apart by
time.

10

No
other
life

but
this
grows

old
and
stiff.

11

If nature never refused
any resentment
rings true in whose
heart fear
rankles far and wide,

and if birds and beasts
bereft of soul
hold no consolation but
honey and balm,
forgotten sundrenched rise,

then grief's crushing curve
returns to earth
our happy home begets no
joy despite each
parched swirl of verse,

nor lamenting bitter never
to come but coddled
starspilled night awakes
another sudden
day a new one says I.

12

And raised eyes skyward
to rebuke sorrow so
benign becomes
hateful spite
of life in
defense of which
none should under
stand all unrequited

signs as laurel leaves
given to rifled light
or darkest line
released
and recoiled
from easy scorn
craves what's not
more than what may be.

13

May those who
loom with stark tales
of torment told
to control any soul
stranded on
ways without heart

burn limbsplayed
in their own
bad dreams undying
empty minds
fleecing those who
strive for life.

But when power
unmasked becomes
power undone;
when, laid flat by love,
one overcomes
despair and wanders

willingly without shame
or fear, finding
pain true as beauty,
then no image
awaits everlasting
dread to come.

14

Entangled
earth verse,
vexed of forever,
fashioned of matter
both body and soul means
to end in unmeasured death;
recompose us as embryonic
starroot, severed from
every beginning not
seized by gravity is
saved by life's
pyrelight.

May 2000—November 2001

Note

I began *Arranging Nature* while reading Lucretius' *On the Nature of Things* as a way of thinking through the question of what it might mean to approach nature in poetry in the 21st century. The trace of that reading remains present in parts one and three of this book, which draw a good deal of their language from Lucretius' poem. As one pagan to another, I trust he won't mind.

About the Author

Paul Naylor's books of poetry include *Playing Well With Others* (Singing Horse Press, 2004) and *Book of Changes* (Quarry Press, 2000). He is also the author of *Poetic Investigations: Singing the Holes in History* (Northwestern University Press, 1999), a study of five contemporary poets. His poems and essays have appeared in *Boston Review, Boxkite, Chicago Review, Contemporary Literature, Cross-Cultural Poetics, Golden Handcuffs Review, Hambone, New American Writing, New Orleans Review,* and *Postmodern Culture.*

Recent and new books from Chax Press

Kass Fleisher, *Accidental Species*
Tenney Nathanson, *Erased Art* (New West Classics 5)
Heather Nagami, *Hostile*
Caroline Koebel and Kyle Schlesinger, *Berlin Schablone*
Linh Dinh, *American Tatts*
Patrick Pritchett, *Burn: Doxology for Joan of Arc*
Jonathan Brannen, *Deaccessioned Landscapes*
David McAleavey, *Huge Haiku*
Norman Fischer, *Slowly but Dearly*
Keith Wilson, *Transcendental Studies* (New West Classics 4)
Beverly Dahlen, *A-Reading Spicer & 18 Sonnets* (New West Classics 3)
David Bromige, *As in T As in Tether* (New West Classics 2)
Nathaniel Tarn, *The Architextures* (New West Classics 1)
Nick Piombino, *Hegelian Honeymoon*
Jerome Rothenberg, *A Book of Concealments*
Bill Lavender, *While Sleeping*
Elizabeth Treadwell, *Chantry*
Allison Cobb, *Born Two*
Todd Baron, *TV Eye*
Karen Mac Cormack, *Implexures*
Pierre Bettencourt, *Fables*
Heather Thomas, *Resurrection Papers*
Nathaniel Mackey, *Four for Glenn*
Charles Bernstein, *Let's Just Say*
Hank Lazer, *Deathwatch for My Father*
Mark Weiss, *Figures: 32 Poems*

For additional titles please visit our web site: http://www.chax.org